The Boosey & Hawkes Piano Sonata Collection

CONTENTS

BÉLA BARTÓK
3 Sonata

LEONARD BERNSTEIN
28 Sonata

AARON COPLAND
45 Piano Sonata

ALBERTO GINASTERA
72 Sonata No. 1, Op. 22

SERGEI PROKOFIEV
97 Sonata No. 3, Op. 28

IGOR STRAVINSKY
110 Sonata

ISBN 978-1-4584-1760-2

BOOSEY & HAWKES

AN IMAGEM COMPANY

DISTRIBUTED BY

HAL•LEONARD®
CORPORATION
7777 W. BLUEMOUND RD. P.O. BOX 13819 MILWAUKEE, WI 53213

T0050661

www.boosey.com
www.halleonard.com

Notes on the Sonatas

BÉLA BARTÓK (1881-1945)
Sonata

Composed in 1926, the same year as piano works *Out of Doors* and *Nine Little Piano Pieces*. Bartók began his six-volume series *Mikrokosmos* in 1926 (completed in 1939). Sonata was first performed on December 8, 1926, in Budapest, Hungary, by the composer. New edition of Sonata revised by Peter Bartók in 1992.

LEONARD BERNSTEIN (1918-1990)
Sonata

Composed in 1938, the same year as piano work *Music for the Dance No. II*. Written for Heinrich Gebhard. First performed in 1938 in Boston, Massachusetts, by the composer.

AARON COPLAND (1900-1990)
Piano Sonata

Composed 1939-1941 in the time between ballets *Billy the Kid* (1938), *Rodeo* (1942), and *Appalachian Spring* (1943-1944). Commissioned by Clifford Odets. First performed on October 21, 1941, in Buenos Aires, Argentina, by the composer.

ALBERTO GINASTERA (1916-1983)
Sonata No. 1, Op. 22

Composed in 1952, during Ginastera's subjective nationalist period. Commissioned by the Carnegie Institute and the Pennsylvania College for Women for the 1952 Pittsburgh International Contemporary Music Festival. First performed on November 29, 1952 at Carnegie Music Hall in Pittsburgh, Pennsylvania, by Johana Harris.

SERGEI PROKOFIEV (1891-1953)
Sonata No. 3, Op. 28

Composed in 1917, during the same period as piano works *Visions fugitives* (1915-1917) and Sonata No. 4 (1917). Opus 28 was based on material from an earlier piano work, Sonata No. 3 (1907).

IGOR STRAVINSKY (1882-1971)
Sonata

Composed in 1924, during the same period as piano work *Serenade in A* (1925). First performed on July 16, 1925, in Donaueschingen, Germany, by Felix Petyrek.

SONATA
for Piano

BÉLA BARTÓK
(1926)

I

10

(4' 20")

II

* Muffle the sound suddenly on pedal and key

(4' 30")

III

Allegro molto, ♩ = 170

Duration: ca. (12' 30")

Dittának, Budapesten, 1926, jun.

for Heinrich Gebhard (in memoriam)

SONATA
for the piano

LEONARD BERNSTEIN
(1938)

I.

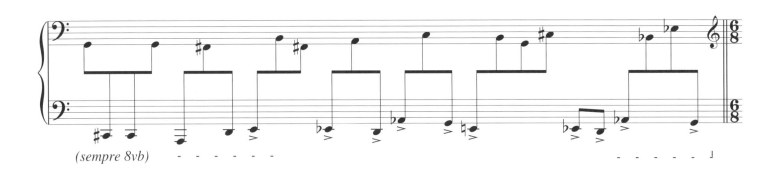

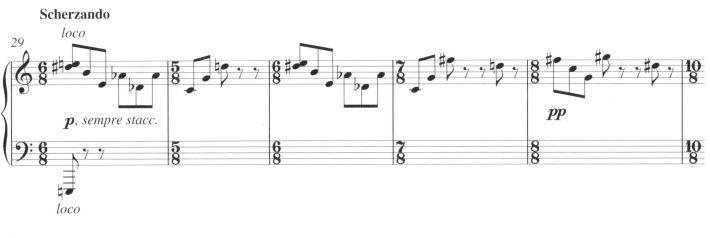

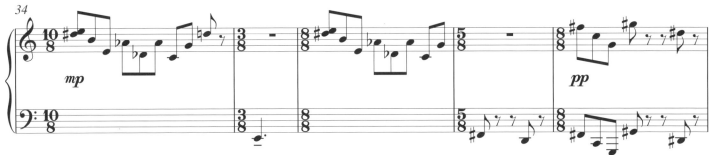

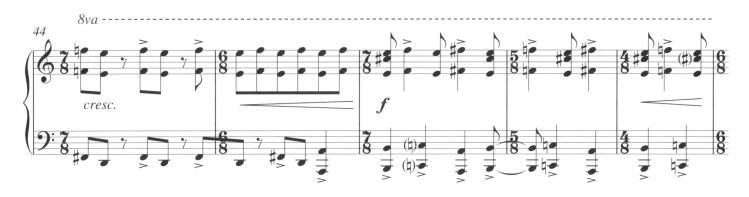

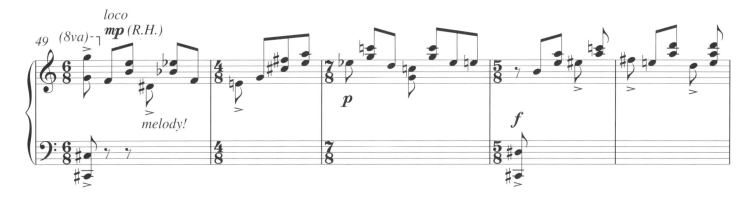

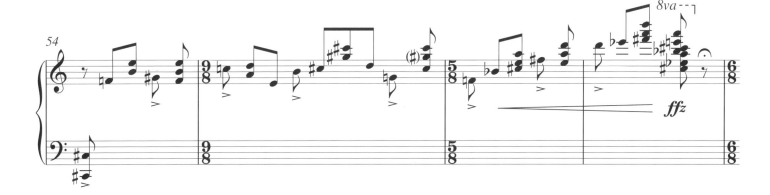

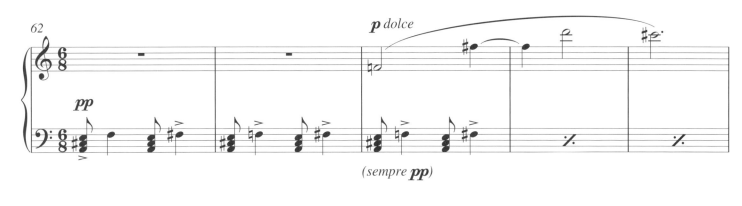

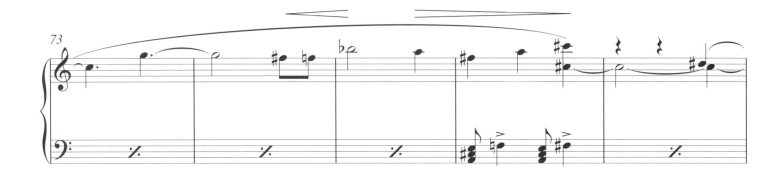

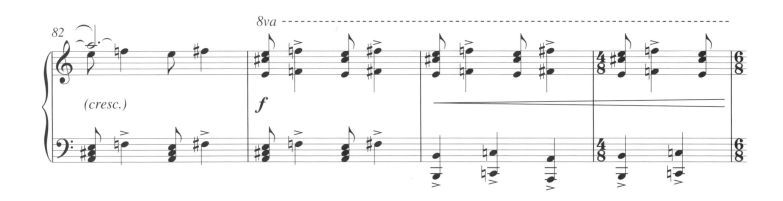

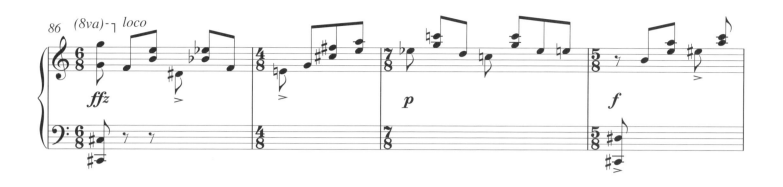

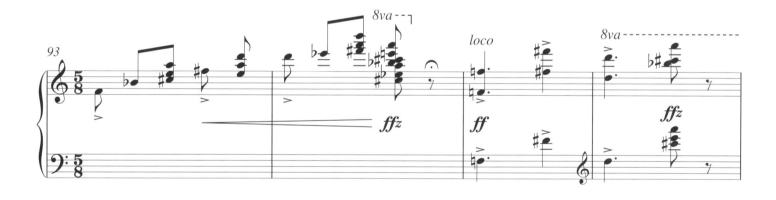

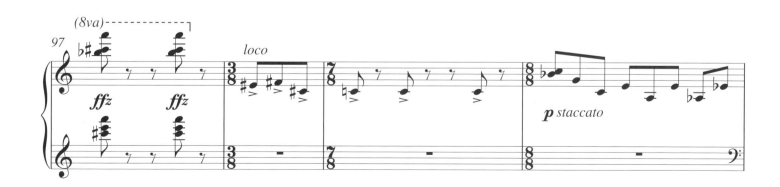

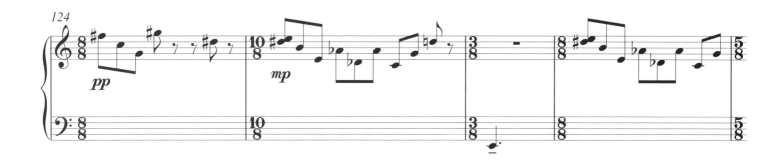

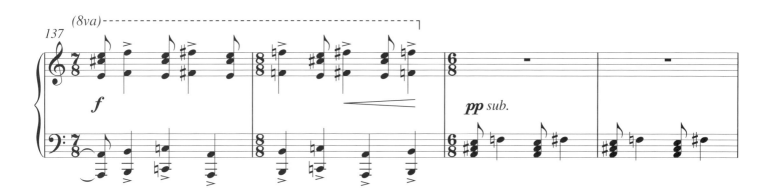

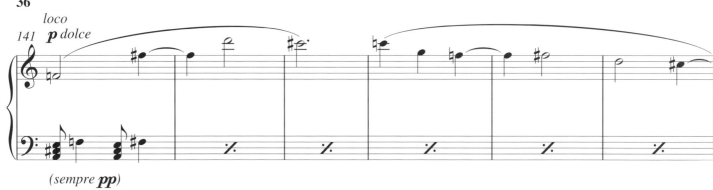

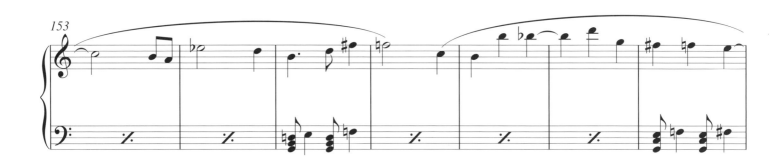

II.

112 *The time values indicated in this cadenza are only approximate to what is psychologically correct.*

To Clifford Odets

PIANO SONATA

AARON COPLAND
(1939-1941)

a Johana y Roy Harris

SONATA NO. 1

ALBERTO GINASTERA
Op. 22
(1952)

I

II

III

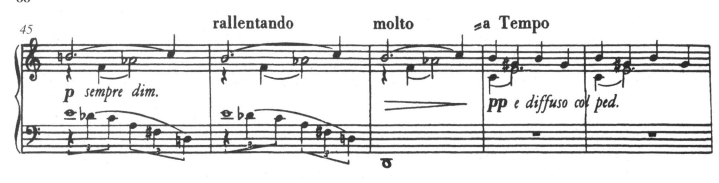

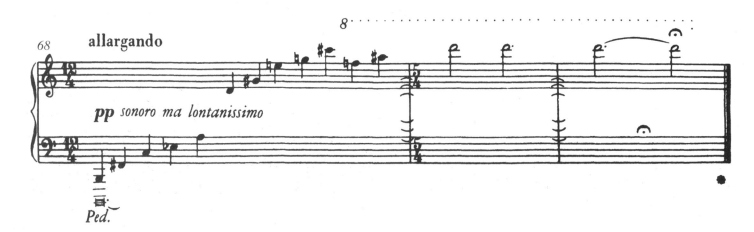

IV

92

This page intentionally left blank to facilitate page turns.

To Mr. Boris Werin

SONATA NO. 3
(D'APRES DES VIEUX CAHIERS)

SERGEI PROKOFIEV
Op. 28
1917 (1907)

104

Dédiée à Madame la Princesse Edmond de POLIGNAC

SONATA

1

Edited by
ALBERT SPALDING
(New York)

IGOR STRAVINSKY
(1924)

112

x

3

staccatissimo